Testimonials

I feel like someone, has at last, stepped inside the inner shadows of my own heart and shined a light over the disarray. Rather than retreating further, I felt myself relaxing, even laughing at the thought that someone else understands, and has found a way into true freedom.

Jillian Brooker

This is a most unusual and a most wonderful book. These poems have burst forth from a well of healing, each one alive and energised by its unique voice to bring weeping, laughter, deep peace... understanding and beauty. Lie back, read, listen and drink deeply of the Love that will come softly and unexpectedly.

Elizabeth Aplin

Luce's poems are honest and kind. In them you will find a healing, nourishing treat for your soul.

Aaron Nebauer

This poetry beautifully expresses the Journey of Loves coming whose both soft and dramatic, almost violent action, takes us to the place of peace where Love dwells.

Bronwyn Van Bockel

audio recording from artist available on
……..website

This book holds the potential to:

1. Germinate the seeds of Love that are already planted in you.

2. Create pathways of hope and strategy.

3. Awaken you to the substance, immediacy, and power of Love.

4. Awaken you to your higher purpose.

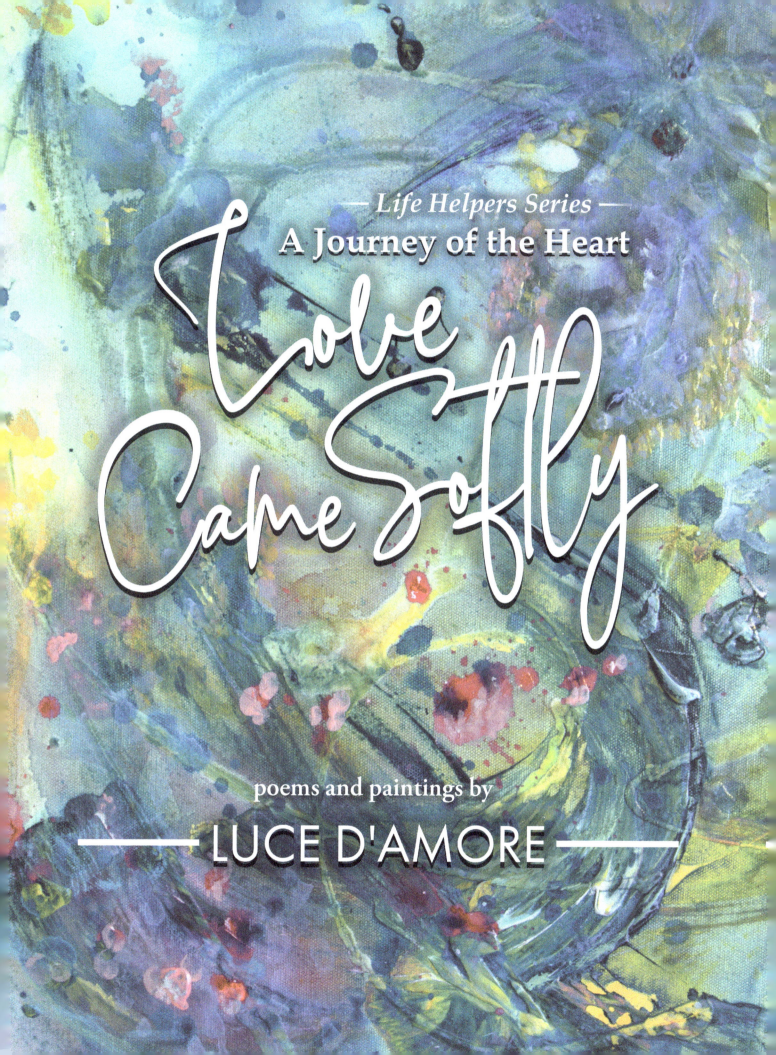

Love Came Softly
Copyright © 2019 by LUCE D'AMORE

All rights reserved. No part of this publication may be reproduced, distributed, or transmitted in any form or by any means, including photocopying, recording, or other electronic or mechanical methods, without the prior written permission of the author, except in the case of brief quotations embodied in critical reviews and certain other non-commercial uses permitted by copyright law.

Tellwell Talent
www.tellwell.ca

ISBN
978-0-2288-2112-0 (Hardcover)
978-0-2288-2111-3 (Paperback)
978-0-2288-2113-7 (eBook)

Table of Contents

The Journey

Dedicated To 10
Foreword 11

Follow Me

The Invitation 13
When I had given up 16
Snow began to fall 18
I learned early 21

The Tempest

Don't tell me what to do 25
The arrow 28
The fortress 30
Grief 32

Grieving

The hand-me-down 36
The Heart of Love 38
The pimple on a hill 40
The pox 42
Love slapped me in the face 45

Embers Of Love In My Heart

Pathways..51
The rescue 53
A crack appeared…..56
Love came… and carried me away!...59

Hope

Love wouldn't let me go..63
The crowd 65
The fragment..68
Footsteps 70
I remembered 72

Strong Roots Pushing Upwards Towards Life

The highway 76
Hugs 79
Oh no it's Monday!..81

Breaking Through

What they told us..84
Murmurings...87
Wave after wave 89

Waves

There's a time……...92
Who we are in Love..95
The new library...97

Spreading Out To Shade Others

The horse whisperer 100
How beautiful 103

Drinking At Loves Table

The Cornerstone 107

Acknowledgements 109

Love

is a

PERSON

Because of language restrictions,

I refer to this PERSON as

IT

a backward acronym for

This Intelligence.

The Journey

Dedicated To

My children,

their families,

and future generations.

May you come to know this Love in far greater ways that

I would have thought possible and respond to the call.

Those that have not yet begun The Journey;

Those on The Journey,

especially those who are discouraged and tired;

And those who have finished one Journey

and begun another.

May we all sit together at Love's table and tell our adventures

and tales of redemption

and raise our glasses together

to celebrate and honour Love,

the Beginning and the End of every adventure and all that there is.

Foreword

This book is about my personal experiences with Love
and how Love has found a Way to bring me Home.

My greatest desire
is that a whole generation will come to
KNOW the Love
that has brought us into being.

How to use this book:

Read and let Love speak to you.

Buy a copy for someone in need.

Start a group of like-minded people and support one another.

Let Love lead you Home.

Start a Love revolution!

Follow Me

a journey into the unknown

The Invitation

Love came and said

'Follow Me'

I was ill-prepared for The Journey

I had no idea

how arduous it would be

how long the road was

how many mountains had to be climbed

how many cuts and bruises I would get on the Way

and that it would require everything of me

I had no idea

that every part of my being had to be operated on

and so much had to be removed

I had no idea

that no one would understand

this incessant demand of Love

to rearrange and reformat everything

I had no idea

that I was going into foreign territory

to experience in my life

adventures akin to *The Matrix, The Lord of the Rings, Star Wars,* and more!

I had no idea

there were worlds and realities to be conquered

only to be led back to the beginning

to start a new Adventure!

I had no idea

and I'm so very glad!!!

When I had given up

Love came softly

when I least expected it

when I had given up on everything

and all the doors were barred

the paths broken and in disrepair

and sinkholes were appearing at my front door

IT led me out

one footstep at a time

through minefields

and thick ravines

through flooded crocodile-infested waters

and through back alleys

of disreputable neighbourhoods

until at last I was on even ground

hearing the sound of children playing

smells of pizza wafting by

and music coming out of a third-storey window

past flowers

opening up in gardens

to offer their beauty and scent

and then down a lane

to a small cottage with potted flowers

and a welcome mat

Love then took up residence

and I could hear IT rocking

on the front porch

humming and playing the harmonica

stabilizing everything with ITs Presence

Love had brought me Home

Snow began to fall

Snow began to fall

it came before I understood anything about

winter

it didn't stop

it covered everything

then everything began to freeze

no matter what I did to stay warm

it still chilled my bones and marrow

and then my heart

everything went cold

and then the lights went out

the stars too were hidden

by a blanket of doom

and even a simple thing like breathing
became hard to do

I seemed to have entered the darkness
and the darkness had taken up residence in me

even the memory
that there could be another season
was gone and erased

then
just as imperceptibly

the air grew warmer
and I began to breathe more deeply
expanding the space inside

the rays of the sun
began to thaw me out
even down to bone and marrow

seeds of Love

that had been planted in my heart

from the Beginning

began to sprout

and sing joyous songs of new life

enabling me to change the landscape

and run out into the fields to play

and sing songs of hope

to those still trapped and frozen

waiting to be awakened

I learned early

I learned a lot growing up

I learned it wasn't safe to show up
to hold my heart open
to have feelings
to be vulnerable
to be feminine
to need affection

I learned early in life
that I was there to meet
other people's needs
to make them look good

I was disposable
depending on their mood
I did not register
on their to-do list
it was already full with their own needs

My voice was not heard

and I soon learned to be invisible

I learned to rely on myself

to meet my own needs

and to bury everything left over

I learned to be in control

and to keep everyone at bay

and then to top it all off

I learned to forget

Then Love came

and taught me to remember

and I learned with Love

how to unlock the hidden

compartments of my life

and find those parts of myself

that I had locked away

welcoming them in my arms

and holding them in Love

I learned to love myself

and then Love began

to spill onto others

and in the end

the circle was complete again

Love had found a way

to restore everything

and somehow

weave a rich tapestry

of dark and vibrant colours

interwoven with golden threads

a deeply satisfying

landscape of redemption

The Tempest

Don't tell me what to do

Don't tell me what to do
it's my way or the highway

Don't tell me what to do
I know I'm right

Don't tell me what to do
these well-built walls are there for a reason

Don't tell me what to do
I've been out of control
and now I'm taking it back

Don't tell me what to do
I've shut myself down
can't hear the cries or feel the tears

Don't tell me what to do

I've removed the windows and the doors

and cemented myself in

I shout out from my tower

with my hard hat and bulletproof vest

shooting rounds of ammunition

from my unrestrained vocals

Don't tell me what to do

it's too late and I don't care anymore

Don't tell me what to do

where were you when I needed you

Meanwhile my true Self

is left alone in the basement

sometimes sobbing uncontrollably

sometimes staring at blank walls

my real Voice unheard

walled up and kept silenced

even from myself

Heard only by Love

who sits silently in the room

waiting to be acknowledged

The arrow

It hit me like an arrow
piercing my chest
fragmenting my life and time
into shattered pieces

Thrust through in a moment of time
sending shocks backwards and forwards
through my timeline

Placing me on a path of shifting platforms
always trying to regain balance
while juggling shattered pieces of my life

Then a second arrow hit my heart
released by the Heavenly Archer

just as powerful

powerful shock waves radiating out

steadying my juggling

and my footsteps

pulling everything back into ITself

pulling everything back into the Source

to the Centre

to the Beginning

The fortress

I had built a fortress
with a moat full of crocodiles
with minefields and keep-out signs
enter at own risk!!!

Hot oil pouring out of windows
and expert archers at the walls

I lived in bunkers, underground
out of reach, out of sight
SAFE
I thought, in my cocoon

And then Love
brazenly walked in
and air lifted me out

How's that

I had to be rescued

from my own protection!

Love built walls with windows

and doors around me

and taught me to direct traffic

IT filled my home with flowers

music and paintings

rugs and comfy pillows

IT built a picket fence

with a gate

and designed a flower

and vegetable garden

IT brought in new visitors

and then somehow

transplanted all this into my heart

so that I could live in Eden

and manifest it on Earth

Grief

Grief like a mighty river

that had somehow been dammed up

began to overflow its banks

and began to wash over me

like a torrent

threatening to rip the fabric

of my heart and chest

wanting to escape

to find a way out to sea

to find its resting place

I had ignored it for so long

damned it up

even without my knowing

and now it seemed to threaten my very existence

with a pent-up force

I had not experienced before

Tearing apart walls and barriers

I had erected to wall it in

now easily uprooted

and carried away

My chest feeling hollowed-out

my eyes still holding back

this river

this torrent

the pent-up emotion

of a thousand years

Till at last

the sobs that convulsed my being

were able to expel

this raging monster

that I had created

and I finally landed on the shore

peaceful at last

back in the arms of Love

Grieving

The hand-me-down

They sent in the troops
thinking I had gone berserk

what were they thinking!
this is my normal state

erratic, out of control, isolated,
quiet, spaced out, not coping

a revolving door of states
up, down, around

being cycled through a heavy wash
in a rough washing machine

spat out, still soaking wet
and pulled out of shape

thrown into a dryer that's too hot

that keeps changing its mind

which way to go

rough hands pulling me out

and throwing me in the corner

like a discarded hand-me-down

left till mildew begins to form

then, one day, out of the blue

some stranger comes in

hand-washes me

in lavender and frankincense

blow-dries me ever so tenderly

and wears me like a trophy

like something hard-won from a huge battle

honoured to display me

on ITs heart of Love

The Heart of Love

Mesmerized
like a deer trapped in headlights
or like children watching TV

on the outside looking in
stuck, not able to move

a glass wall separating me from the action
always observing but never entering in

in a silent world where my screams
could not be heard
and my cries for help unanswered
smiling and angry faces looking but not seeing

accompanied only by my own reflection in the glass
abandoned there by humanity
serving a life sentence
for what they had done

me, myself, and I
keeping one another company
reading magazines on holiday destinations
and how to renovate igloos

Then one day
someone with a child's heart
someone who had not lost connection
with the Heart of Love

somehow managed to walk through the glass
and leave Love behind

making a pathway
through unseen barriers
reconnecting me to Life

The pimple on a hill

Here I am high and dry
stuck like a pimple on top of a hill
baking in the sun

people driving over me
to see the view

here I am
stuck without legs

drying out in the hot sun
wondering what the heck I am doing here
like an obnoxious boil waiting to erupt

spoiling the view from space
listening to the stars singing at night
their voices unnoticed and unheard

wondering what the heck I am doing here

listening to their song

and looking into eternity

without legs to run away

staring into the mysteries

being washed softly by their song

being restored and reclaimed

until legs I didn't know I had

stand up and take me Home

The pox

It's hard to be civil and happy and kind
when pimples are screaming on top of our face
they make a mess and leave their mark
and leave us to play a different part

the stares, the looks, the shuns, the jokes
they leave a mark way down below
so now marked inside and out

our vision starts to change
our image distorted
and those of others too!

the pox
comes in many different packages
some more devastating than others

the result

we see ourselves and others

as objects to be scorned and derided

I sleep, I wake

Now looking through different eyes

with eyes of compassion

I see scarred bodies, hearts, and lives

waiting to be seen through different eyes

eyes that see the hidden treasure

the hidden strength

the hidden juxtapositions and complexities

the beauty behind the veil

the vulnerability behind the anger

the hope behind the despair

the love behind the hatred

the eyes of Love that can pry open

the shell and bring forth the pearl

that has formed there in the darkness

It's these eyes that finally declare and shout

It's over now!

Come out and shine

Love slapped me in the face

I was sitting with my friends

in front of a cold fire

telling familiar stories

and embellishing the facts

hurt, pain, hate, mistrust, revenge

grief, rejection, abandonment

my constant companions

always telling tales in familiar voices

Then Love walked in

slapped me in the face

and rudely pulled me up

and thrust me out

My familiar friends were put out as well

they clung to me as if I was their only home

Love walked in front of me
shining a Light
I could see nothing but a few steps ahead

how can this Love compel me to follow

so many voices complaining
and pointing fingers

I'm in unfamiliar territory
it's steep and arduous

it's heavy going keeping up with Love
IT doesn't stop to consider
the hangers-on I'm carrying!

IT pushes ever relentlessly up the hill
I complain and throw tantrums
words and feelings I never knew I had
come out to assail Love

but IT's indifferent to my barrages
and keeps calling me higher

then just when I'm exhausted

and enraged

and at the end of myself

IT turns around and takes off ITs cloak

revealing a Fire of Love and Purity

embers of this Love fall into my heart

bringing warmth and the glow of Love

making my familiar friends rather uncomfortable

they begin to lose their grip

but are determined to cling on

Then without a word Love jumps off a precipice

and just keeps walking

It's offensive, with no regard for my fears

what am I to do now!

I jump, silent screams of fear

resounding and echoing in me

amazingly I land on Love

who has returned to catch me

I notice that a few of my familiar friends

didn't make the jump

before I can ask any questions

we're off again

Here I am on this adventure with Love

kicking and screaming and complaining

yet compelled

the embers of this Love

taking over my heart

until we're scaling cliffs

and rafting in white water

exhilarated by this adventure

New friends have joined me

joy, peace, laughter, courage

my heart is now on fire

and I find myself slapping

unsuspecting strangers

and pulling them into this wild adventure

this Love is uncontrollable

IT demands to be let out!

Catch the Fire!

Embers Of Love In My Heart

Pathways

Pathways, pathways
Never-ending pathways
of Life and Love

intricately interwoven
in the very fabric of Life
and all that exists

ready to be unlocked
by those awakened
by their call

those ready to receive
their message
to be taught and instructed
and to be led back

to the Beginning

to the Source

to the Voice

to the Light

to Love

The rescue

They said it was too hard
and I would never get out

all the experts got together
looked at all the plans and possibilities
did risk assessments, financial assessments
and possibility assessments

in the end
they hung up their hats
shut down their computers

and left me there
a million miles underground

with no possibility of escape
with meagre supplies

with one little ray of light

that would appear for two hours every day

sometimes I could see what looked like a star

twinkle in the night

silence

and the dripping of Water

were my companions

until the wisdom of Water

led me down not up

deeper into the darkness

deeper into the labyrinth of cavities

where the waters ran

through crevices

and cathedral rooms

through tunnels and channels

down waterfalls

and finally into the River

that knew the way out

and carried me with Love

into the Light

A crack appeared...

Slowly, ever so slowly
a crack appeared
in the dark recesses of my mind

Light peering in for the first time
it was painful at first
causing me to recoil and pull back

then slowly, ever so slowly
I began to enjoy and look forward
to the warmth of ITs glow

IT seemed to make sense
of things I never understood
and battle doubts and fears
until they disappeared

IT began to erode the darkness

the crack seemed to get bigger
ever so slowly

the Light eventually ushered in
Love
a totally unexpected guest
IT sat there holding my misguided hand

somehow communicating
as if by some ancient path
how it was meant to function

then left leaving a deposit of ITs Wisdom
a memory of how things should be

my hand then
unbeknown to me
and without my direction
began to widen the crack
digging, scraping, searching
reaching out

seeking more Light, more Life, more Love

pulling me out

single-handedly

pulling me inside out and upside down

until I was recalibrated

pushing like a sprouting seed

upward and downward

into realms of Light

and into rich soil of nourishment

Wow!

what a hand can do

when it is held by Love!

Love came... and carried me away!

Love came softly

when I least expected it

found a way into my heart

uninvited

passionate about redeeming every part of my fragmented soul

unabated in ITs pursuit

in spite of all my arguments and objections

IT began opening closets

and shining ITs Light in cockroach-infested places

bringing out old photos and punching gloves

rearranging everything

adamant about what had to be thrown out

I would slam doors shut in ITs face

but IT always found a way past my defences

singing soft Love songs

that would awaken long-forgotten places

still bleeding silently in the dark

why so persistent

why so unrelenting

let me hold on to those punches and knife wounds

that give me a right

to blowtorch

those that dare come near

and you

how dare you

as a consuming fire

walk right in

unnerved by my fury

you sit down

and begin to burn away

volumes of well-versed rhetoric

that keeps me stuck in destructive mode

and then proceed to open up my wounds

and scrape them with your Love

now

with anointed wounds

bandaged

I lie in your arms

resting

such a fight

such a struggle

to let Love in

Love came softly

and carried me away!

Hope

Love wouldn't let me go

Love came softly one day
when I was minding my own business
reading a Book

it pulled me into ITself
and wouldn't let me go

IT opened my eyes
all of my eyes
especially the eyes of my heart

IT restrung my tune
and awakened my true song

who knew after so many
blind alleys and incorrect maps

that Love was there all along

interfacing with everything

holding everything together

speaking loudly to every molecule of my being

drowned out by my own indifference

and the cluttered sounds

of those living in forgetfulness

The crowd

Softly softly with unheard footsteps
Love came unannounced
without fanfare
making ITs way through the crowd
of angry screaming faces

Taking my hand gently
and leading me away

leading me to places I had never known
quiet places of refreshment and restoration

whispering things I had never heard before
into my heart
restoring my soul

leading me to pools of still clear water
which reflected a tranquility
I had never known before

and somehow transferring it into my aching soul

pouring liquid oil carrying

a thousand scents and voices

to recalibrate every voice

and everything that screamed at me

from another reality

recalibrating everything

and somehow pouring one realm into another

One look from Love

and everything would jump to attention

and somehow slot into its right place

turning chaos into a masterful jigsaw puzzle

that displayed order in every situation

with beauty and victory clasping

every piece in its right place

majesty like a frame holding it all in place

reformatting the broken pieces of my heart

breathing wholeness and life into every corner of my being

Ready to go back now

and face the angry crowd and speak

Peace Peace

The fragment

I don't want to be here anymore
it's been too long
it's been too hard

I've been trapped in this small space

I can't move
I can't breathe

there's no time here

I'm trapped in the eternal now
trapped in a millisecond
that becomes an eternity

frozen in time and space
a fragment
ejected into space

waiting to be reclaimed

waiting for someone to hear
my frozen scream

then thaw me out in Love
and reclaim me as their own

Footsteps

Soft footsteps came

soft and very loud

cracking the ground they stepped on

causing Light to come through the cracks

Walking through the hard-baked

layers of my soul

encrusted with the hardness

of the generations

that had gone before me

Soft footsteps

that descended into basements

full of bones and relics

letting in Light and air wherever they stepped

Soft footsteps

that found stairways

to forbidden places

and sealed stargates shut

Soft footsteps

that rearranged all the combinations

to the Rubik's Cube of my life

and ushered in a new reality

of never-ending possibilities

Soft footsteps

footprints of Love

that terraformed my life

I remembered

I remembered
deep in the recesses of my mind
the memory of blue skies

With rays of honey
dripping from the sun
feeding lush meadows
of green grass and wildflowers

I remembered
deep in the recesses of my mind
swaddling clothes and rocking chairs
laughter, music, and buttermilk
flowing freely

I remembered
deep in the recesses of my mind
safety and strong walls
with pretty windowpanes
and intricately carved wooden doors

I remembered

deep in the recesses of my mind

soft lush thick carpets and fireplaces

the aroma of freshly baked cookies

and dinner simmering on the stove

Memories from another Life

another Homeland

another Beginning

that seeped into the grey walls

of my existence

drawing me back

out of the squalor

out of the emptiness

lifting me up from bare wooden floors

to the possibility

of another Life

causing me to rip back the layers

the walls

the partitions

until I could once again

enter Love's Home

and feed from her joyous abode

Strong Roots Pushing Upwards Towards Life

The highway

It's funny who we meet on the highway

little old ladies with a skip in their step

youth with vacant faces and hollowed eyes

well-dressed business people running after a paper trail

exasperated parents

singles wanting a partner

and couples wanting to be single

heartache, backache, sinuses, and cancer

Signposts everywhere pointing to the Way

covered over with ads

products, vacations, new cars

the latest technology to make us happy

and of course 'You deserve it!'

pavement strewn with broken hopes and dreams
shattered lives and relationships

caring people with wheelbarrows
picking up the broken pieces
of humanity left behind

preachers on soap boxes
with politically correct and incorrect messages

ears plugged into beats
to drown out
the stillness, the silence, the place of reflection

Love comes and leaves a calling card
no one is ever home to open the door
and so it goes unnoticed

relegated to the junk mail pile
deemed too costly to entertain
and much too disruptive to invite in

yet love keeps knocking

having all the keys to our hearts and lives

waiting to be noticed and invited in

Hugs

Some people hug like they want to keep you at bay

Some hug mechanically
not really inhabiting their bodies

Some hug pretending to give
but really getting their needs met

Some hug patronizingly

Some hug from a heart of Love
landing kisses that give Life

And then
there are those who
envelop you in arms of Love
to draw you into their heart

and somehow germinate a thousand seeds of Love

that explode within you

gluing the pieces of your broken life

back together

this is Love

that has found a dwelling place

and has at last

found hearts and arms

to do ITs bidding

Oh no it's Monday!

Oh no it's Monday!
the weekend has slipped by
gear up, start up, move up
run here, go there, shop here

revolving doors churning out the days

here we are it's Friday

catch up on the chores, get drunk
get laid, fill the fridge, wash the car
party hard, sleep in, sleep out

Oh no it's Monday!

I fall out of bed, out of my window
into a different realm
I can live in time but it makes room for me

I'm in touch with what needs to happen

I'm in the flow

I make meaningful contact with Life

and those around me

I pour out and receive back

there's meaning and design

moments of intimacy

and exchanges of Love

I have discovered a place of

Rest and Flow

Come all you that are heavy laden

and I will give you Rest

Breaking Through

What they told us

They told us it was OK

to use our bodies any which way

doll them up, sex them up

drown them down, paint them black

or just go out wearing a hat

wear them out

trample them down

lug them around

use and abuse them

what the heck

But wait

what if eternity wanted to break out and live here

having veiled ITself and constrained ITself

holding ITself back

waiting to see if anyone noticed

if anyone was awake

willing to be insulted, defiled, and misused

in the hope of being recognized

honoured and embraced

What if Love

had wanted a place to dwell

a place to interface

a place of divine exchange

a meeting place

a transformation place

a place where heaven and earth meet

What then would we do with this place

that has been given us

this lightning conductor

this alchemical wonder

that changes everything

What then?

Murmurings

Unintelligible words
spoken in foreign languages
that I don't understand

seeping out of my heart and chest
rumblings and bloatings
growling in my gut
unformulated groans

Murmurings always murmurings
describing worlds I have not yet
consciously encountered

telling me tales of wonders I have not yet
perceived with my senses

calling me deeper into another realm
pulling me across galaxies
back to my Source

connecting me deeper

into the Voice

that speaks a million languages

in one sound, one note

that harmonizes with ITself

and recalibrates all things

Murmurings always murmurings

of tales yet to be fulfilled

calling me deeper

calling me higher

unwrapping and enfolding

Murmurings always murmurings

will I answer the call……

Wave after wave

Wave after wave

came pounding at my door

some good, some bad, some indifferent

but they all took their toll

I wasn't built for this constant assault

I wanted to escape, to opt out

wave after wave

wanting to knock me over

and drag me out to sea

as they retreated

And then Love came
and took me to Higher ground
and taught me to rule the waves
and to command the waters

harnessing their power and intent
And now, like an expert rider
I've learned to ride the waves

channelling them into profitable paths
to bring forth Life

creating pathways of Life and Hope
for those still pounded by the waves

Waves

There's a time......

There's a time to dance
and a time to be still and contemplate

a time for exuberant joy
and a time for grief and letting go

a time to shout from rooftops
and a time for intimate whispers

a time to be lost in someone's eyes
and a time to give them the look

a time for hearts to be open
and a time for hearts to be protected

a time for spring cleaning
and a time to gather and store memories

a time when the heart wants to sing

and a time when the heart wants to be sung to

a time when knees are strong

and a time when knees buckle

a time when feet run on petalled roads

and a time to dawdle kicking autumn leaves

a time to feel the breeze

running through one's fingers

and a time for fingers to wipe away tears

a time to sit and watch children playing

and a time to join them

a time to indulge in freshly baked cake

and a time to give one's piece to another

a time to storm the halls

and a time to walk in solitude

a time to notice those around

and a time to notice oneself

in all these times

Love presents ITself

it's time to notice Love

Who we are in Love

Bushes

have you noticed

everyone hides behind bushes

jobs

clothes

makeup

titles

wealth

ideologies

behind cleverly designed roles

rescuer

controller

victim

behind elaborate masks

that deceive even ourselves

behind so many bushes

that in the end

we can't even find ourselves

And then

Love comes

and invites us to walk

naked and unashamed

knowing that who we are in Love

is more than enough

The new library

Softly softly without a shadow of a doubt
Love picked me up and carried me away

It was confusing at first
whizzing past so many unfamiliar landscapes
trees, mountains, and waterfalls
boulders and rocks

a feast to the senses
after never-ending shrubs

mists in the morning
and golden peaks at sunset

like a new library of words unfolding
new languages holding volumes of books

experiences and lives unfolding effortlessly
speaking of eras and ages and things to come

rumbling in monotones like railway engines

pulling a heavy load

and humming like birds enjoying the sunshine

rays of light piercing through the clouds

and sounds of water gurgling and sliding

and leaping over rocks

and then

just as softly

I was carried back

with this new library of sounds and colours

a smorgasbord of life

back to the scrub

to touch everything anew

and bring something new forth

never seen before

Spreading Out To Shade Others

The horse whisperer

Quietly

imperceptibly

almost like IT had always been there

Love came

I had to notice and press into IT

nuzzle into IT

get to know IT

breathe IT in

Like a horse whisperer

gaining the trust of a horse

except that I was the horse

not wanting to be tamed

not wanting to lose my 'freedom'

wanting to bolt and run away

but somehow being held there

by this irresistible Love

gentle and firm

trustworthy yet quite other

wanting relationship

wanting partnership

wanting me to keep my will

and yet willingly yielding myself

so that somehow

we would ride as one

knowing each other's thoughts

and feeling each other's feelings

moving even at full speed

as one

somehow both being changed

forming something unique and new

two wills working together

pulling on each other's heartstrings

creating a beautiful symphony

outworked in unison and trust

I had found a new kind of freedom!

How beautiful

How beautiful are those
whose hearts have been cleansed
whose feet have been washed

Who have learned to walk with Love
stooping ever so low
to pick up the broken pieces of humanity
and to restore them
as they have been restored

How beautiful are those
who have abandoned themselves to Love
who have followed Love
to all the 'wrong' places
to see the restoration of all things

How beautiful are those

who by beholding Love

have learned to hold out

their hearts and arms

to restore creation

to Love's original intent

How beautiful are those

who have laid aside everything

to follow this Love

into darkness and existential death

to be raised up again

as bright shining stars

How beautiful are those

who have lost themselves in Love

and found not only themselves

but the true nature of all things

revealed to them

How beautiful are those

who follow the Way

back to the Beginning

to manifest the End

and begin a New Beginning

Drinking At Loves Table

The Cornerstone

There's a Cornerstone
that needs to be beheld

There's an Ancient Path
that needs to be followed

There's a Door
that's been set in place

There's a Way a Truth and a Life
that leads us there

There's a Love that beckons us
and a Voice that calls us by name

to enter in

to behold

to be transformed

and to hold all things together

through our Love

Acknowledgements

I would like to acknowledge my daughter Elisa who has been on her own Journey and has accompanied me on mine and has sacrificially financially sown into this book.

I would like to acknowledge those that have been on this adventure with us and have also financially sown into this book.

I would like to acknowledge my dear friend Paul Pfeiffer whose Journey has crossed with mine and who has photographed my paintings with much care!

I would also like to thank John, Rhea and the Tellwell team for making this new adventure so effortless!

Lightning Source UK Ltd.
Milton Keynes UK
UKHW050720211119
353961UK00005B/19/P